PIONEER VALLEY EDUCATIONA

BIG
AND SMALL

ROSE LEWIS

Look!

The bone is big.

Look!

The kitten is small.

Look!
The ball is big.

Look!

The fish is small.

Look!

The shoes are big.

Look!

The dog is small.

Look!

The   lollipop   is   big.

small
fish

small
dog

small
kitten

big
shoes

big
ball

big
bone

big
lollipop